The Batsford Book of Sporting Verse

The Batsford Book of
SPORTING VERSE

Edited by Peter Verney

B. T. BATSFORD LTD, LONDON

First published 1979
Copyright Peter Verney 1979

Printed in Great Britain by
The Garden City Press,
Letchworth, Hertfordshire
for the Publishers B. T. Batsford Ltd,
4 Fitzhardinge Street, London W1H 0AH
ISBN 0 7134 2009 X

Contents

Introduction

This is a book for a winter's fireside, when the wind
blows, the traffic rumbles and the peace of the river, the
tingle of the flight or the sustained excitement of the chase
can be only dreams.

Any choice is bound to be invidious and a choice of poetry
no more nor less than any other, but in this selection I
have tried to evoke and capture the spirit and the moment
of sport. Some better known verse I have left out; some
less well known I have included. Some will miss their own
favourites, but I hope that every reader will find in these
pages some new delight, or find again one that had been
forgotten for too long.

HUNTING

On Shank's Nag

I never yet owned a horse or a hound,
I never was lord of a foot of ground,
Yet few are richer, I'll be bound,
   Than me of a hunting morning.

I'm far better off than he that pays,
For, though I've no money, I live at my ease,
With hunting and shooting, whenever I please,
   And a tally-i-ho in the morning.

As I go on foot I don't lose my seat,
As I take the gaps I don't break a gate,
And if I'm not first, I am seldom late,
   With my tally-i-ho in the morning.

And there's not a man, be he high or low,
In the parts down here, or wherever you go,
That doesn't like poor old Tipparary Joe,
   With his tally-i-ho in the morning.

Anonymous Hunting Song

Hunting Song

Stags in the forest lie, hares in the valley-o!
  Web-footed otters are spear'd in the lochs;
Beasts of the chace are not worth a Tally-ho!
  All are surpassed by the gorse-cover fox!
    Fishing, though pleasant,
    I sing not at present,
    Nor shooting the pheasant,
      Nor fighting of cocks;
    Song shall declare a way
    How to drive care away,
    Pain and despair away,
      Hunting the fox!

Bulls in gay Seville are led forth to slaughter, nor
  Dames in high rapture, the spectacle shocks;
Brighter in Britain the charms of each daughter, nor
  Dreads the bright charmer to follow the fox.
    Spain may delight in
    A sport so exciting;
    Whilst 'stead of bull-fighting
      We fatten the ox;
    Song shall declare a way
    How to drive care away,
    Pain and despair away,
      Hunting the fox!

England's green pastures are graz'd in security,
  Thanks to the Saxon who car'd for our flocks!
He who reserving the sport for futurity,
  Sweeping our wolves away left us the fox.
      When joviality
      Chases formality,
      When hospitality
        Cellars unlocks;
      Song shall declare a way
      How to drive care away,
      Pain and despair away,
        Hunting the fox.

R. E. Egerton Warburton (1804–1891)

The Stable Path

The last red rose on the arch has faded,
  The border has mourned for its last white flower;
The dahlias droop where the frost has raided,
  The grass is wet with the autumn shower;
Dull are the paths with their leaf-strewn gravel,
  Cold is the wind as it wanders by,
Still there's a path that a man can travel
  Happy at heart though the roses die.

The path to the stable! – Though summer be ended,
  Though down through the garden no bird be astir,
This path has new melodies tunefully blended –
  The flick of a whip with the clink of a spur!
So – on through the yew-trees where shadows strike chiller,
  Across the paved court-yard, at last to the stall
Where, pawing in eagerness, chained on the pillar
  Stands, champing his bit-bars, the Pearl of them All!

Will H. Ogilvie (b. 1869)

Bolts

I've a head like a violin-case; I've a jaw like a piece of steel;
I've a mouth like india-rubber, and devil a bit I feel;
So I've had my fun with a biped thing that clambered upon my
  back,
And I'm in at the death, though I'm panting for breath, right
  bang in the midst of the pack.

With a cockney sportsman mounted on top,
That has hired me out for the day,
  It's the moment for me to be off for a spree
  In a new and original way.
  In my own most original way.
  Oats! but my spirits were gay!
When I betted my bit that my rider should sit
  Somewhere else ere the close of the day.

I started a gentle canter; I felt him bob about,
His spurs went in, and the roots of sin, they whipped my hind
  legs out.
He put his arms around my neck, 'twas kindly meant, I swear,
But he had no call to spoil it all by pulling out half my hair.

He left his hat in a puddle, he left his whip on a gate,
The briars knew where, but I don't care, the bits of his tunic
  wait;
He bade me stay, I raced away, to the sound of the huntsman's
  horn,
And at last I laid him gently in the arms of a bold blackthorn.

The whip waits safe in the harness-room, the groom in the
  stable yard,
It's not that I mind a tanning – my hide's grown far too hard –
But that tied to a fly I'm safe to die, and on chaff and straw
  abstain,
For sure as I snort, if they give me this sort, of course I shall do
  it again.

With a cockney sportsman mounted on top,
That has hired me out for the day
It's the moment for me to be off for a spree
In a new and original way.
In my own most original way.
Oats! but my spirits were gay!
When I betted my bit that my rider should sit,
Somewhere else ere the close of the day.

Anonymous

Lord Epsom

A Horse Lord Epsom did bestride
With mastery and quiet pride.
He dug his spurs into its hide.
The Horse, discerning it was pricked,
Incontinently bucked and kicked,
A thing that no one could predict!

Lord Epsom clearly understood
The High-bred creature's nervous mood,
As only such a horseman could.
Dismounting, he was heard to say
That it was kinder to delay
His pleasure to a future day.
        .   .   .   .   .

He had the Hunter led away.

Hilaire Belloc (1870–1953)

19

The Good Grey Mare

Oh! once I believed in a woman's kiss,
  I had faith in a flattering tongue,
For lip to lip was a promise of bliss,
  When lips were smooth and young.

But now the beard is grey on my cheek,
  And the top of my head gets bare,
So little I speak, like an Arab scheik,
  And put my trust in my mare.

For loving looks grow hard and cold,
  Fair heads are turned away,
When the fruit has been gathered, the tale been told,
  And the dog has had his day.
But chance and change 'tis folly to rue,
  Say I, the devil may care!
Nor grey nor blue is to bonny and true
  As the bright brown eye of my mare.

It is good for the heart that's chilled and sad
  With the death of a vain desire,
To borrow a glow that shall make it glad
  From the warmth of a kindred fire.
And I leap to the saddle, a man indeed!
  For all I can do and dare,
In the power and speed that are mine at need
  While I sit on the back of my mare.

With the free, wide heaven above outspread,
  The free, wide plain to meet,
With the lark and his carol high over my head,
  And the bustling pack at my feet,
I feel no fetter, I know no bounds,
  I am free as a bird in the air,
While the covert resounds in a chorus of hounds
  Right under the nose of the mare.

We are in for a gallop! Away! away!
    I told them my beauty could fly,
And we'll lead them a dance ere they catch us to-day,
    For we mean it – my lass and I!
She skims the fences, she scours the plain,
    Like a creature winged, I swear,
With snort and strain on the yielding rein;
    For I'm bound to humour the mare.

They have pleached it strong; they have dug it wide;
    They have turned the baulk with the plough,
The horse that can cover the whole in its stride
    Is cheap at a thousand I vow!
So I draw her together, and over we sail,
    With a yard and a half to spare!
Bank, bull-finch, and rail, it's the curse of the Vale!
    But I leave it all to the mare.

Away! away! they've been running to kill!
    With never a check from the find.
Away! away! we are close to them still,
    And the field are furlongs behind!
They can hardly deny they were out of the game,
    Lost half 'the Fun of the Fair',
Though the envious blame, and the jealous exclaim,
    'How that old fool buckets his mare!'

Who-whoop! They have him! They're round him; how
    They worry and tear when he's down!
'Twas a stout hill-fox when they found him; now
    'Tis a hundred tatters of brown!
And the riders, arriving as best they can,
    In panting plight declare,
'That first in the van was the old grey man
    Who stands by the old grey mare.'

I have lived my life; I am nearly done;
  I have played the game all round;
But I freely admit that the best of my fun,
  I owe it to horse and hound.
With a hopeful heart and a conscience clear
  I can laugh in your face, Black Care!
Though you're hovering near, there's no room for you here,
  On the back of my good grey mare.

G. J. Whyte-Melville (*1821–1878*)

The Whipper-in

From the cradle his name has been 'Hard-riding Dick'
Since the time when cock-horse he bestraddled a stick;
Since the time when, unbreech'd, without saddle or rein,
He kick'd the old jackass along the green lane.

Dick, wasting no time o'er the classical page,
Spent his youth in the stable without any wage;
The life of poor Dick when he enter'd his 'teens,
Was to sleep in the hayloft and breakfast on beans.

Promoted at length, Dick's adventures began: –
A stripling on foot, but when mounted a man;
Capp'd, booted and spurr'd, his young soul was on fire,
The day he was dubb'd 'Second Whip' to the Squire.

See, how Dick, like a dart, shoots ahead of the pack!
How he stops, turns, and twists, rates, and rattles them back!
The laggard exciting, controlling the rash,
He can comb down a hair with the point of his lash.

O! show me that country which Dick cannot cross –
Be it open or wood, be it upland or moss,
Through the fog or the sunshine, the calm or the squall,
By daylight or starlight, or no light at all!

Like a swallow can Dick o'er the water-flood skim,
And Dick, like a duck, in the saddle can swim;
Up the steep mountain-side like a cat he can crawl,
He can squeeze like a mouse through a hole in the wall!

He can tame the young wild one, inspirit the old,
The restive, the runaway, handle and hold;
Sharp steel or soft-sawder, which e'er does the trick,
It makes little matter to Hard-riding Dick.

Bid the chief from the Desert bring hither his mare,
To ride o'er the plain against Dick if he dare;
Bring Cossack or Mexican, Spaniard or Gaul,
There's a Dick in our village will ride round them all!

A whip is Dick's sceptre, a saddle Dick's throne,
And a horse is the kingdom he rules as his own;
While grasping ambition encircles the earth,
The dominions of Dick are enclosed in a girth.

Three ribs hath he broken, two legs, and one arm,
But there hangs, it is said, round his neck a life-charm;
Still, long odds are offer'd that Dick, when he drops,
Will die, as he lived, in his breeches and tops.

R. E. Egerton Warburton (*1804–1891*)

The Whip

As, still as a statue, he sits on his horse,
    Watching and waiting,
Or rounding up stragglers behind in the gorse,
    Cursing and rating,
He's always the same, hard-bitten and game.

The voice of a hound, or the click of a hoof
    Tell him what's doing,
He knows, on the instant, alert and aloof,
    All that is brewing;
Lean-visaged and tanned, he's always at hand.

When hounds are at fault and are lifted in vain,
    Nothing resulting,
His musical holloa is heard through the rain,
    Faintly exulting;
He's sure to be right, whatever the plight.

And, during a run, when the pack, in full cry,
    Goes hell-for-leather,
He sees, all the time, with his critical eye,
    Hounds are together;
No matter the pace, he's there in his place.

But, after its over, we leave in our cars,
    Cosily weary,
While he collects hounds by the light of the stars,
    Placidly cheery;
Although it's hard work, there's nothing he'd shirk.

And, if, every day, he is up with the dawn,
    Grooming and feeding,
There'll come a time, soon, when he'll carry the horn,
    True to his breeding;
The salt of the earth, he'll show what he's worth.

Edric Roberts

The Opening Run

The rain-sodden grass in the ditches is dying,
  The berries are red to the crest of the thorn;
Coronet-deep where the beech leaves are lying
  The hunters stand tense to the twang of the horn;
Where rides are re-filled with the green of the mosses,
  All foam-flecked and fretful their long line is strung,
You can see the white gleam as a starred forehead tosses,
  You can hear the low chink as a bit-bar is flung.

The world's full of music. Hounds rustle the rover
  Through brushwood and fern to a glad 'Gone away!'
With a 'Come along, Pilot!' – one spur-touch and over –
  The huntsman is clear on his galloping grey;
Before him the pack's running straight on the stubble –
  'Toot-toot-too-too-too-oot!' – 'Tow-row-ow-ow-ow!'
The leaders are clambering up through the double
  And glittering away on the brown of the plough.

The front rank, hands down, have the big fence's measure;
  The faint hearts are craning to left and to right;
The Master goes through with a crash on The Treasure,
  The grey takes the lot like a gull in his flight.
There's a brown crumpled up, lying still as a dead one;
  There's a roan mare refusing, as stubborn as sin,
While the breaker flogs up on a green underbred one
  And smashes the far-away rail with a grin.

The chase carries on over hilltop and hollow,
  The life of Old England, the pluck and the fun;
And who would ask more than a stiff line to follow
  With hounds running hard in the Opening Run?

Will H. Ogilvie (b. 1869)

The Find

Yon sound's neither sheep-bell nor bark,
They're running – they're running. Go hark!
The sport may be lost by a moment's delay;
So whip up the puppies and scurry away,
Dash down through the cover by dingle and dell,
There's a gate at the bottom – I know it full well;
And they're running – they're running,
        Go hark!

They're running – they're running. Go hark!
One fence and we're out of the park;
Sit down in your saddles and race at the brook,
Then smash at the bullfinch; no time for a look;
Leave cravens and skirters to dangle behind;
He's away for the moors in the teeth of the wind,
And they're running – they're running,
        Go hark!

They're running – they're running. Go hark!
Let them run on and run till it's dark!
Well with them we are, and well with them we'll be,
While there's wind in our horses and daylight to see:
Then shog along homeward, chat over the fight,
And bear in our dreams the sweet music all night
Of – They're running – they're running,
        Go hark!

Charles Kingsley (1819–1875)

The Galloping Squire

Come, I'll show you a country that none can surpass,
  For a flyer to cross like a bird on the wing,
We have acres of woodland and oceans of grass,
  We have game in the autumn and cubs in the spring,
We have scores of good fellows hang out in the shire
But the best of them all is the Galloping Squire.

The Galloping Squire to the saddle has got,
  While the dewdrop is melting in gems on the thorn,
From the kennel he's drafted the pick of his lot,
  How they swarm to his cheer! How they fly to his horn!
Like harriers turning or chasing like fire,
'I can trust 'em, each hound!' says the Galloping Squire.

One wave of his arm to the covert they throng,
  'Yoi! wind him! and rouse him! By Jove! he's away!'
Through a gap in the oaks see them speeding along,
  O'er the open like pigeons, 'They *mean* it today!
You may jump till you're sick – you may spur till you tire!
For it's catch 'em who can!' says the Galloping Squire.

Then he takes the old horse by the head and he sails,
  In the wake of his darlings, all ear and all eye
As they come in his line, o'er banks, fences and rails
  The cramped ones to creep, and the fair ones to fly.
It's a *very* queer place that will put in the mire,
Such a rare one to ride as the Galloping Squire.

But a fallow has brought to their noses the pack,
  And the pasture beyond is with cattle-stains spread,
One wave of his arm, and the Squire in a crack
  Has lifted and thrown in his beauties at head.
'On a morning like this, it's small help you require,
But he's forward, I'll swear!' says the Galloping Squire.

So forty fair minutes they run and they race,
    'Tis heaven to some! 'tis a lifetime to all,
Though the horses we ride are such gluttons for pace,
    There are stout ones that stop, there are safe ones that fall,
But the names of the vanquished need never transpire,
For they're all in the rear of the Galloping Squire.

Till the gamest old varmint that ever drew breath,
    All stiffened and draggled, held high for a throw,
O'er the Squire's jolly visage, is grinning in death,
    Ere he dashes him down to be eaten below;
While the daws flutter out from a neighbouring spire
At the thrilling who-whoop of the Galloping Squire.

And the labourer at work, and the lord in his hall,
    Have a jest or a smile when they hear of the sport,
In ale or in claret he's toasted by all,
    For they never expect to see more of the sort.
And long may it be ere he's forced to retire,
For we breed very few like the Galloping Squire.

G. J. Whyte-Melville (1821–1878)

A Rum One to Follow,
A Bad One to Beat

Come, I'll give you the health of a man we all know,
  A man we all swear by, a friend of our own,
With the hounds running hardest, he's safest to go,
  And he's always in front, and he's often alone.
A rider unequalled – a sportsman complete,
A rum one to follow, a bad one to beat.

As he sits in the saddle, a baby could tell
  He can hustle a sticker, a flyer can spare,
He has science, and nerve, and decision as well,
  He knows where he's going and means to be there.
The first day I saw him they said at the meet,
That's a rum one to follow, a bad one to beat.

We threw off at the Castle, we found in the holt,
  Like wildfire the beauties went streaming away,
From the rest of the field he came out like a bolt,
  And he tackled to work like a schoolboy to play,
As he rammed down his hat, and got home in his seat,
This rum one to follow, this bad one to beat.

'Twas a caution, I vow, but to see the man ride!
  O'er the rough and the smooth he went sailing along;
And what Providence sent him, he took in his stride,
  Though the ditches were deep, and the fences were strong.
Thinks I, 'If he leads me I'm in for a treat,
With this rum one to follow, this bad one to beat!'

Ere they'd run for a mile, there was room in the front,
  Such a scatter and squander you never did see!
And I honestly own I'd been out of the hunt,
  But the broad of his back was the beacon for me.
So I kept him in sight, and was proud of the feat,
This rum one to follow, this bad one to beat!

Till we came to a rasper as black as your hat,
    You couldn't see over – you couldn't see through,
So he made for the gate, knowing what he was at,
    And the chain being round it, why – over he flew!
While I swore a round oath that I needn't repeat,
At this rum one to follow, this bad one to beat.

For a place I liked better I hastened to seek,
    But the place I liked better I sought for in vain;
And I honestly own, if the truth I must speak,
    That I never caught sight of my leader again.
But I thought, 'I'd give something to have his receipt,
This rum one to follow, this bad one to beat.'

They told me that night he went best through the run,
    They said that he hung up a dozen to dry,
When a brook in the bottom stopped most of their fun,
    But I know that I never went near it, not I.
For I found it a fruitless attempt to compete
With this rum one to follow, this bad one to beat.

So we'll find him a bumper as deep as you please,
    And we'll give him a cheer, for deny it who can,
When the country is roughest he's most at his ease,
    When the run is severest he rides like a man.
And the pace cannot stop, nor the fences defeat,
This rum one to follow, this bad one to beat.

  G. J. Whyte-Melville (*1821–1878*)

The Veteran

He asks no favour from the Field, no forward place demands,
Save what he claims by fearless heart and light and dainty hands;
No man need make a way for him at ditch or gap or gate,
He rides on level terms with all, if not at equal weight.

His eyes are somewhat dimmer than they were in days of yore,
A blind fence now might trap him where it never trapped before;
But when the rails stand clean and high, the walls stand big and
    bare,
There's no man rides so boldly as there's no man rides so fair.

There is no other in the Field so truly loved as he;
We better like to see him out than any younger three;
And yet one horseman day by day rides jealous at his rein –
Old Time that smarts beneath the whip of fifty years' disdain.

He crowds him at his fences, for he envies his renown;
Some day he'll cross him at a leap and bring a good man down,
And Time will take a long revenge for years of laughing scorn,
And fold the faded scarlet that was ne'er more nobly worn.

Here's luck! Oh! good, grey sportsman! May Time be long defied
By careful seat and cunning hand and health and heart to ride,
And when that direful day be come that surely shall befall,
We'll know you still unbeaten, save by Time that beats us all!

Will H. Ogilvie (b. 1869)

Tally-Ho!

There are soul-stirring clouds in the fiddle and flute,
  When dancing begins in the hall,
And a goddess in muslin, that's likely to suit,
  Is the mate of your choice for the ball;
But the player may strain every finger in vain,
  And the fiddler may rosin his bow,
Nor flourish nor string such a rapture shall bring,
  As the music of sweet Tally-Ho!

There's a melody, too, in the whispering trees
  When day has gone down in the West,
And a lullaby soft in the sigh of the breeze
  That hushes the woods to their rest;
There are madrigals fair in the voices of air,
  In the stream with its ripple and flow,
But a merrier tune shall delight us at noon,
  In the music of sweet Tally-Ho!

When autumn is flaunting his banner of pride
  For glory that summer has fled,
Arrayed in the robes of his royalty, dyed
  In tawny and orange and red;
When the oak is yet rife with the vigour of life,
  Though his acorns are dropping below,
Through bramble and brake shall the echoes awake,
  To the ring of a clear Tally-Ho!

'A fox, for a hundred!' they know it, the pack,
  Old Chorister always speaks true,
And the Whip from his corner is told to come back,
  And forbid to go on for a view.
Now the varmint is spied, as he crosses the ride,
  A tough old campaigner I trow –
Long, limber, and grey, see him stealing away
  – Half a minute! – and then – Tally-Ho!

Mark Fanciful standing, all eye and all ear,
    One second, ere wild for the fun,
She is lashing along with the pace of a deer,
    Her comrades to join in the run.
Your saddle you grip, gather bridle and whip,
    Give your hunter the office to go,
In his rush through the air little breath is to spare
    For the cheer of your wild Tally-Ho!

At the end of the wood the old farmer in brown,
    On the back of his good little mare,
Shows a grin of delight and a jolly bald crown,
    As he holds up his hat in the air;
Though at heart he's as keen as if youth were still green,
    Yet (a secret all sportsmen should know)
Not a word will he say till the fox is away,
    Then he gives you a real Tally-Ho!

There's a scent, you may swear, by the pace that they drive,
    You must tackle to work with a will,
For as sure as you stand in your stirrups alive,
    It's a case of a run and a kill!
So I wish you good speed, a good line, and a lead,
    With the luck of each fence where it's low,
Not the last of the troop, may you hear the Who-Whoop,
    Well pleased as you heard Tally-Ho!

G. J. Whyte-Melville (1821–1878)

Running On

The dusk is down on the river meadows,
   The moon is climbing above the fir,
The lane is crowded with creeping shadows,
   The gorse is only a distant blur;
The last of the light is almost gone,
    But hark! They're running!
      They're running on!

The count of the year is steadily growing;
   The Old give way to the eager Young;
Far on the hill is the horn still blowing,
   Far on the steep are the hounds still strung
Good men follow the good men gone;
    And hark! They're running!
      They're running on!

Will H. Ogilvie (b. 1869)

A Single Hound

When the opal lights in the West had died
   And night was wrapping the red ferns round,
As I come home by the woodland side
   I heard the cry of a single hound.

The huntsman had gathered his pack and gone;
   The last late hoof had echoed away;
The horn was twanging a long way on
   For the only hound that was still astray.

While, heedless of all but the work in hand,
   Up through the brake where the brambles twine,
Crying his joy to a drowsy land
   Javelin drove on a burning line.

The air was sharp with a touch of frost,
   The moon came up like a wheel of gold;
The wall at the end of the woods he crossed
   And flung away on the open wold.

And long as I listened beside the stile
   The larches echoed that eerie sound:
Steady and tireless, mile on mile,
   The hunting cry of a single hound.

Will H. Ogilvie (b. 1869)

The King of the Kennel

Clara fuga, ante alios, et primus in aequore pulvis

The bitch from the Belvoir, the dog from the Quorn,
The pick of their litter our puppy was born;
And the day he was entered he flew to the horn,
But rating and whipcord he treated with scorn.
    Gently, Bachelor,
    Have a care! Have a care!

So eager to find, and so gallant to draw,
Though a wilder in covert a huntsman ne'er saw.
'Twas a year and a half ere he'd listen to law,
And many's the leveret hung out of his maw.
    Ware hare, Bachelor;
    Ware hare! Ware hare!

On the straightest of legs and the roundest of feet,
With ribs like a frigate his timbers to meet,
With a fashion and fling and a form so complete,
That to see him dance over the flags is a treat!
    Here, here, boy! Bachelor!
    Handsome and good.

But fashion and form without nose are in vain;
And in March or mid-winter, storm, sunshine, and rain,
When the line has been foiled, or the sheep leave a stain,
His fox he accounts for again and again.
    Yooi! Wind him, Bachelor.
    All through the wood!

He guides them in covert, he leads them in chase;
Though the young and the jealous try hard for his place,
'Tis Bachelor always is first in the race;
He beats them for nose, and he beats them for pace.
    Hark forward to Bachelor!
    From daylight to dark!

Where the fallows are dry, where manure has been thrown,
With a storm in the air, with the ground like a stone –
When we're all in a muddle, beat, baffled, and blown,
See! Bachelor has it! Bill, let him alone.
    Speak to it, Bachelor;
    Go hark to him! Hark!

That time in December – the best of our fun –
Not a mile from the gorse, ere we'd hardly begun,
Heading straight to the river – I thought we were done;
But 'twas Bachelor's courage that made it a run.
    Yooi! over, Bachelor!
    Yooi! over, old man!

As fierce as a torrent, as full as a tank,
That a hound ever crossed it, his stars he may thank!
While I watched how poor Benedict struggled and sank!
There was Bachelor shaking his sides on the bank.
    Forrard on, Bachelor!
    Catch ye who can.

From the find to the finish, the whole blessed day,
How he cut out the work! How he showed us the way!
When our fox doubled back where the fallow-deer lay,
How he stuck to the line, and turned short with his prey!
    Yo-Yooite, Bachelor!
    Right, for a crown!

Though so handy to cast, and so patient to stoop,
When his bristles are up you may swear it's who-whoop!
For he'll dash at his fox like a hawk in her swoop,
And he carries the head, marching home to his soup!
    Sess! Sess! Bachelor,
    Lap and lie down.

    G. J. Whyte-Melville (1821–1878)

The Place Where the Old Horse Died

In the hollow by the pollard, when the crop is tall and rank
  Of the dock leaf and the nettle growing free,
Where the bramble and the brushwood straggle blindly o'er the
    bank,
  And the pyat jerks and chatters on the tree,
      There's a fence I never pass
      In the brushwood and the grass,
    But for very shame I turn my head aside,
      While the tears come thick and hot
      And my curse is on the spot –
  'Tis the place where the old horse died.

There's his hoof upon the chimney, there's his hide upon the
    chair,
  A better never bent him to the rein;
Now, for all my love and care, I've an empty stall and bare;
  I shall never ride my gallant horse again!
      How he laid him out at speed,
      How he loved to have a lead,
    How he snorted in his mettle and his pride!
      Not a flyer of the Hunt
      Was beside him in the front,
    At the place where the old horse died.

Was he blown? I hardly think it. Did he slip? I cannot tell.
  We had run for forty minutes in the vale,
He was reaching at his bridle; he was going strong and well,
  And he never seemed to falter or to fail;
      Though I sometimes fancy, too,
      That his daring spirit knew
    The task beyond the compass of his stride,
      Yet he faced it true and brave
      And dropped into his grave,
    At the place where the old horse died.

I was up in half a minute, but he never seemed to stir,
  Though I scored him with my rowels in the fall;
In this life he had not felt before the insult of the spur,
  And I knew that it was over once for all.
    When motionless he lay,
    In his cheerless bed of clay,
  Huddled up without an effort on his side –
    'Twas a hard and bitter stroke,
    For his honest back was broke
  At the place where the old horse died.

With a neigh so faint and feeble that it touched me like a groan,
  'Farewell' he seemed to murmur, 'ere I die';
Then set his teeth and stretched his limbs, and so I stood
  alone,
While the merry chase went heedless sweeping by.
    Am I womanly and weak
    If the tear was on my cheek
  For a brotherhood that death can thus divide?
    If sickened and amazed
    Through a woeful mist I gazed
  On the place where the old horse died?

There are men both good and wise, who hold that in a future
      state,
  Dumb creatures we have cherished here below,
Shall give us joyous greeting when we pass the golden gate;
    Is it folly that I hope it may be so?
      For never man had friend
      More enduring to the end,
    Truer mate in turn of time and tide.
      Could I think we'd meet again
      It would lighten half my pain
    At the place where the old horse died.

G. J. Whyte-Melville (1821–1878)

Tom Moody

You all knew Tom Moody, the whipper-in, well;
The bell just done tolling was honest Tom's knell;
A more able sportsman ne'er followed a hound,
Through a country well known to him fifty miles round.
No hound ever open'd with Tom near the wood,
But he'd challenge the tone, and could tell if 'twere good;
And all with attention would eagerly mark,
When he cheer'd up the pack, 'Hark! to Rookwood, hark! hark!
    High! – wind him! and cross him;
    Now, Rattler, boy! – Hark!'

Six crafty earth-stoppers, in hunter's green drest,
Supported poor Tom to an 'earth' made for rest;
His horse, which he styled his Old Soul, next appear'd,
On whose forehead the brush of the last fox was rear'd;
Whip, cap, boots, and spurs, in a trophy were bound,
And here and there follow'd an old straggling hound.
Ah! no more at his voice yonder vales will they trace,
Nor the welkin resound to the burst in the chase!
    With High Over! – now press him!
    Tally-ho! – Tally-ho!

Thus Tom spoke to his friends ere he gave up his breath,
'Since I see you're resolved to be in at the death,
One favour bestow – 'tis the last I shall crave –
Give a rattling view-hollow thrice over my grave;
And unless at that warning I lift up my head,
My boys you may fairly conclude I am dead!'
Honest Tom was obey'd, and the shout rent the sky,
For every voice join'd in the tally-ho cry,
    Tally-ho! Hark forward!
    Tally-ho! Tally-ho!

Andrew Cherry

Hunter Trials

It's awf'lly bad luck on Diana,
    Her ponies have swallowed their bits;
She fished down their throats with a spanner
    And frightened them all into fits.

So now she's attempting to borrow,
    Do lend her some bits, Mummy, *do*;
I'll lend her my own for to-morrow,
    But to-day *I'll* be wanting them too.

Just look at Prunella on Guzzle,
    The wizardest pony on earth;
Why doesn't she slacken his muzzle
    And tighten the breech in his girth?

I say, Mummy, there's Mrs Geyser
    And doesn't she look pretty sick?
I bet it's because Mona Lisa
    Was hit on the hock with a brick.

Miss Blewitt says Monica threw it,
    But Monica says it was Joan,
And Joan's very thick with Miss Blewitt,
    So Monica's sulking alone.

And Margaret failed in her paces,
    Her withers got tied in a noose,
So her coronets caught in the traces
    And now all her fetlocks are loose.

Oh, it's me now. I'm terribly nervous.
    I wonder if Smudges will shy.
She's practically certain to swerve as
    Her Pelham is over one eye.

❖   ❖   ❖   ❖   ❖

Oh wasn't it naughty of Smudges?
   Oh, Mummy, I'm sick with disgust.
She threw me in front of the Judges,
   And my silly old collarbone's bust.

John Betjeman (*1906–*)

Epitaph

Green grows the grass,
O'er the sporting old stager
Who overrode hounds
Of an ex-Indian major.

Anonymous

FISHING

The Angler

Beside a vast and primal sea
A solitary savage be.

Who gathered for his tribe's rude need
The daily dole of raw sea-weed.

He watched the great tides rise and fall,
And spoke the truth – or not at all!

Along the awful shore he ran
A simple pre-Pelasgian;

A thing primeval, undefiled,
Straightforward as a little child –

Until one morn he made a grab
And caught a mesozoic crab!

Then – told the tribe at close of day
A bigger one had got away!

From him have sprung (I own a bias
  To ways the cult of rod and fly has)
All fishermen – and Ananias!

Patrick Chalmers (b. 1874)

The Chavender or Chub

There is a fine stuffed chavender,
  A chavender or chub,
That decks the rural pavender,
  The pavender or pub,
Wherein I eat my gravender,
  My gravender or grub.

How good the honest gravender!
How snug the rustic pavender!
From sheets as sweet as lavender,
  As lavender or lub,
I jump into my tavender,
  My tavender or tub.

Alas, for town and clavender,
  For business and my club!
They call me from my pavender
To-night – ay, there's the ravender,
  Alas, there comes the rub!

To leave each blooming shravender,
  Each spring-bedizened shrub,
And meet the horsey savender,
  The very forward sub,
At dinner in the clavender,
And then at billiards dravender,
  At billiards soundly drub
The self-sufficient cavender,
  The not ill-meaning cub,
Who me a bear will davender
  A bear unfairly dub,

Because I sometimes snavender,
  Not too severely snub,
His setting right the clavender,
  His teaching all the club.

Farewell to peaceful pavender,
  My river-dreaming pub,
To bed as sweet as lavender,
To homely wholesome gravender
And you, inspiring chavender,
  Stuffed chavender or chub.

  W. St. Leger

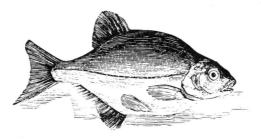

The Cream Of It

'Twixt the primrose and the dog-rose,
   'Twixt the March-Brown and the Drake,
Till young rooks, in gollywog rows,
   Hold the windy elms awake,
Lie the paths that Ariel flits on
   When we dream, in cities mean,
Easter waters, streams at Whitsun,
   And of stolen days between!

Dreams of dark, of northern rivers,
   And the pass still packed with snow
(For the months are stubborn givers
   Where the spring-run salmon show),
Where the North-East storms and blusters,
   Yet the courting grouse cock swanks
And in shy and starry clusters,
   Peeps the primrose on the banks!

Dreams – a flow of crystal wanders
   'Neath the high, wind-haunted chalk,
And the captious pounder ponders
   And the dry-fly pundits stalk;
And an inn there is at even
   Where the brethren sit confessed
Of the Orkneys to Loch Leven,
   From Loch Leven to the Test!

Dreams, where Thames the old, slow speeding,
   Glides through lilac'd hours and gay,
Where the ten-pound trout was feeding
   (So you're told) but yesterday;
Where you check your leisured homing
   (Empty creeled!) to stand and hear
Philomena in the gloaming
   Call the waiting summer near!

Dreams of leisure, dreams of pleasure,
    Dreams that crown their radiant rout
With the Mayfly's mazy measure,
    And a carnival of trout;
Where the cuckoo calls uncaring
    Down the endless afternoon,
And the dog-rose twines his fairing
    On the bonny brows of June!

While the rivers do not falter,
    But run downward to the main,
While the changing seasons alter,
    And the swallow comes again,
While the tadpole to the frog grows
    And the acorn to the tree,
Shall the primrose and dog-rose
    Bind the golden hours for me!

Anonymous (1920)

A Spinning Song

O the hungry day in March
With the roses on the larch!
are plum buds on the alder, and the black upon the ash,
With the river-water green
You are neither heard nor seen,
the wind is netting meshes and the ripples gently splash.

How the rushes hiss and rattle,
And the little catkins prattle!
are white horse foals a prancing, just beyond at Bullimore,
Those with great pipes of waterlilies
Seem to hear the stamping fillies,
unsheathe their sweet green scimitars, and lift them up for war.

Down the wind with rod and traces
to the changeless changing places,
a pocket full of spinners, and a little net and bag;
just a whisper on the margent,
'My device is gules and argent.
and I will follow softly with the spinner that can wag.'

So we cast afar and follow
Where the banks are clear and hollow –
Ha! already? see the rascal is curvetting to the snag,
See, he shakes his angry head,
Now he's sulky. Now he's led,
Quick! the net below his tail and he tumbles in the bag.

So the dappled sunbeams quiver
In the woods below the river,
So the dark weed sways and stretches like the shadow on his back.
Who can dare him? or discern him
In his secret lair? or turn him
In the war dance of his hunger, when his rows of lancets crack?

Charles Marson

April on Tweed

As birds are fain to build their nest
   The first soft sunny day,
So longing wakens in my breast
   A month before the May,
When now the wind is from the West,
   And Winter melts away.

The snow lies yet on Eildon Hill,
   But soft the breezes blow.
If melting snows the waters fill,
   We nothing heed the snow,
But we must up and take our will, –
   A-fishing will we go!

Below the branches brown and bare,
   Beneath the primrose lea,
The trout lies waiting for his fare,
   A hungry trout is he;
He's hooked, and springs and splashes there
   Like salmon from the sea!

Oh, April tide's a pleasant tide,
   However times may fall,
And sweet to welcome Spring, the Bride,
   You hear the mavis call;
But all adown the waterside
   The Spring's most fair of all.

Andrew Lang (1844–1912)

The Gentle Recreation

Then sometime in a dusky evening late;
  A *grey snail* from the ground I take,
  And gently o'r the stream I troul.
  'Tis safe, 'tis sure to try with all,
If but some Rain the day before did fall,
  For Muddy streams a little vext,
  With falling showers decoy him best:
  Or, take a *Beetle* always brown,
That Boys from off the Apple-trees knock down,
Which in an Evening late when all the Stars,
  To Heaven's black Canopy withdraws,
  You may be sure good sport to find,
If but the following precepts well you mind,
Four wings he has, two scaly, two of softest down
But with his tail your largest hook encrown;
Ne'r hurt him, all his Wings he will expand,
And Sing a Murmuring Tune the Trouts can understand,
  Who greedy of so sweet a prey,
Leap straight and bear the Songster quite away.
When with a sudden touch I feel him rove,
I soon injoy my wishes and my Love,
Try this but once, you'll quickly find it true,
And neatly after this same slight persue.
But let no noise the weary Trout offend,
By stiring ground or reeds, lest vaine our wishes end.
    .   .   .   .   .   .

No sooner was compleat my Fishing Geer,
But that I chanc'd to spy unto me steer.
 Two *Carps* that were of mighty size,
My heart e'n leapt to make of one a prize;
As they came Sailing careless on their way,
A well scour'd worm I in their course convay.
 The water there not two foot deep,
  Besides so clear,
That all their motions plainly did appear,
Behind a shady Oak conceal'd I stood,
And with a wary eye observ'd the flood,
 And all their motions as they mov'd,
  Thus while they nearer drew,
  My hopes I still renew,
  They'd nibble at my bait,
Tho after curse me for my sly deceit;
 And quickly plainly cou'd descry,
That one had something pleasing to his eye,
He seem'd to smile and with expanded Jaws,
Hug'd his good luck and silent gave Applause.
Till with a gentle touch I hook'd him streight,
While he stood wondring whence should come deceit,
Under the Luster of so fair a bait;
 He never seem'd, or scorn'd to run,
But with a sudden jerk his tail did turn,
And then as suddenly my Joys were gone,
 For my new strand gave way and broke,
 But what's become of worm and hook,
 For both I'm sure he fairly took,
Vext, no, we Anglers often loose our prize,
Compleat let all our Tackling be, and most precise,
For Fishes prove sometimes more wise than we,
As by this late ensample all may see,

        .   .   .   .   .

63

'Tis pity for to part the *Carp* and he,
Since muddy Ponds with both do well agree;
  One bait doth both delight,
  A worm that's red and bright,
  Excells a Thousand trifling things,
That bungling Anglers to small purpose brings,
    To scare the Fish away:
  Both yield sweet pleasure, both delight,
  Tho both contrary ways do bite,
    And also play,
Carps eager gape and draw the flote downright,
Then when he's hung he runs with all his might
  Nor water beats he with his tail,
  Till life and strength together fail;
The *Tench* he only gently sucks the worm,
And several ways the floting flote will turn,
Until the hook within his Jaws doth lie,
Angler forbear, for that once done to th' reeds he'll ply,
Sinking his prey for to secure and speedy dye.
The gentle touch he'll beat the water with his tail,
Imploring help, no help can then prevail.

·   ·   ·   ·   ·

  Soon from the River then withdraw,
Into some *Farm*, and turn the rotten straw.
For *Worms*, a ruby head and body white,
Are certain signs the *Roach* at them will bite,
Set but a few, you need no more to fear,
But you'll have sport if any *Roach* are there,
I seldom find them at this bait precise;
And some I've ta'en with other *Fishes eyes.*
    One time my baits were spent,
      I thoughtfull was for more,
    When Fortune favour'd my intent,
      And soon supply'd my store;
A sudden fancy in my Nodle came,
    Which I resolved then to try,

Do you but make experience of the same,
   You may succeed as well as I,
The Glaring *Oculus*, great Loves misterious bait,
That leads the World in errour, Topsy turns a state,
Which Monarchs more adore, and brighter shines,
Then all the glittering stones adorn their Diadems:
This was my fancy, and I well may say,
Eyes were my guide the Fishes to betray,
For some I took, *Jove* pardon my Intent
To make the blind decoy the Innocent;
Wonder no more, 'tis certain true and just,
Necessity begot Invention first.

                    .   .   .   .   .   .

If you but one Inch, or rather on the ground,
Your *Bradling* tail, as you the water sound;
   For he'll ne'er rise, try all the Art you can,
   To take a bait that's from the ground a span.
   A *Bradling*, that his chiefest Love,
   A *Gentle*, sometimes will him move.
So will the *Straw-worm*, from his house drawn clear,
Shew you the pleasure that in Rivers are.
         A pliant Rod,
         No sturdy Goad,
      That Rustick People use,
         Gives more delight,
         When *Gudgeons* bite,
      Then all their vain Ostentious shews.
         A Hook that's fine,
         And Taper Line,
      Two or three hairs below,
         May well suffice,
         Unto the wise,
      When they to Angling go.

   John Whitney

The Old Fisher's Challenge

Oh! let it be in April-tide,
But one of April's best,
A mornin' that seems made o' May,
In dews and sunshine drest;
Frae off the Crags o' *Simonside*,
Let the fresh breezes blow,
And let auld *Cheviot's* sides be green,
Albeit his head be snow.

Let the stream glitter i' the sun,
The curl be on the pool,
The rash gale rufflin' aye its face
Aneath the Alder's cool:
Or if the Spring will have her clouds,
Then let them pass me soon;
Or if they take a thought and stay,
Then let it be at noon.

Oh! freshly from his mountain holds
Comes down the rapid *Tyne*;
But *Coquet's* still the stream of streams;
So let her still be mine;
There's many a sawmon lies in *Tweed*,
An' many a trout in *Till*;
But *Coquet* – *Coquet* aye for me,
If I may have my will.

Let it be 'stream an' stream about,'
Or if that mayna be,
Take off old *Coquet* where ye like
From *Thirlmore* to the sea;
But leave to me the streams I love,
The streams that know my hand,
An' 'weight to weight' with the best be
That's in *Northumberland*.

Let me begin at *Brinkburn's* stream,
Fast by the Ruins gray,
An' end at bonny *Eely-haugh*,
Just wi' the endin' day.
My foremost *flee*, the *heckle* red,
My tried Rod springin' free,
An' 'creel to creel' – wi' ony man
In a' the *North Countrie!*

  Thomas Doubleday (*1780–1870*)

The Dove

O my belov'd nymph! fair Dove;
Princess of rivers, how I love
  Upon thy flowery banks to lie
And view thy silver stream,
When gilded by a summer's beam,
  And in it all thy wanton fry
  Playing at liberty,
And with my angle upon them,
  The all of treachery
  I ever learnt, industriously to try!

Charles Cotton (1630–1687)

The Fish

Says John, nodding solemn, 'There's men and there's men,
  And there's some keeps their minds on the latch;
But if ever you pines for to fish down deep,
It's got to be done when you're half asleep,
  And with tackle and hook to match.
And I warn you, James, when you gets a bite,
  It's terrible things you'll catch;
Fishes with goggle eyes, fishes with wings,
Fishes with beards and electric stings,
Shapeless, elastic and jellified things,
  No Christian could despatch!...'

Walter De La Mare (1873–1956)

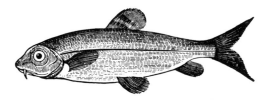

An Angler's Invitation

Come when the leaf comes, angle with me,
Come when the bee hums crossing the lea;
  Come with the wild flowers,
  Come with the mild showers,
Come when the singing bird calleth for thee!

Then to the stream-side gladly we'll hie,
Where the grey trout glide temptingly by;
  Or in some still place,
  Over the hill-face
Cast, ever hoping, the magical fly.

Thomas Tod Stoddart (1810–1880)

Hampshire Fly-Fishing

One, two, three! and the wavy line
    Backward and forward flies,
Four! and there falls, as a gossamer light,
    On the further ring of the rise,
My gay quill-fly, with her wings so dry,
    And she sails on the flowing stream
As a nautilus sails on a summer sea,
    Or a fairy floats in a dream!

    Cotswold Isys (1883)

Eden

When Adam in Eden grew tired o' his life,
Diggin' and delvin', they gied him a wife;
Had they gien him a gaud, wi' a line an' a flee,
Commonsense wad hae keepit him aff o' the Tree;
He wad ne'er hae gane near it ae stap o' his fit,
He micht hae been fishin' the Hiddekel yit!

    'Horace in Homespun'

The Unattainable

I know a pool where the river,
  Sunlit and still,
Slips by a bank of wild roses
  Down from the mill;
There do I linger when summer makes glorious
  Valley and hill.

Somewhere the song of a skylark
  Melts into air,
Butterflies float through the sunshine,
  June's everywhere;
Nature, in fact, shows an amiable jollity
  I do not share.

For in the shade of the alders,
  Scornful of flies,
There is a trout that no cunning
  Coaxes to rise,
Sly as Ulysses, doubtful as Didymus,
  Mammoth in size.

And when the Mayfly battalions
  Flutter and skim,
When all the others are filling
  Baskets abrim,
I spend the cream of a fisherman's carnival
  Casting at him.

Seeing in fancy my hackle
  Seized with a flounce,
Hearing the reel racing madly
  Under his pounce,
Knowing at last all the pounds of his magnitude
  (Eight if an ounce!)

But of my drakes and my sedges
  None make the kill,
None tempt him up from his fastness
  Under the mill,
And, for I saw him as lately as Saturday,
  There he is still.

Thus do Life's triumphs evade us,
  Yet it may be
Some afternoon, when the keeper
  Goes to his tea,
That, if a lob-worm were dropped unofficially –
  Well, we shall see.

Patrick Chalmers (b. 1874)

The Angler's Dinner

Now as an *Angler* melancholy standing
Upon a greene bancke yeelding roome for landing,
A wrigling yealow worme thrust on his hooke,
Now in the midst he throwes, then in a nooke:
Here puls his line, there throwes it in againe,
Mendeth his Corke and Baite, but all in vaine,
He stands long viewing of the curled streame;
At last a hungry *Pike*, or well-growne *Breame*.
Snatch at the worme, and hasting fast away
He knowing it, a Fish of stubborne sway
Puls up his rod, but soft: (as having skill)
Wherewith the hooke fast holds the Fishes gill.
Then all his line he freely yeeldeth him,
Whilst furiously all up and downe doth swimme
Th'insnared Fish, here on the top doth scud,
There underneath the banckes, then in the mud;
And with his franticke fits so scares the shole.
That each one takes his *hyde*, or starting hole:
By this the *Pike* cleane wearied, underneath
A *Willow* lyes, and pants (if Fishes breath)
Wherewith the *Angler* gently puls him to him,
And Least his hast might happen to undoe him,
Layes downe his rod, then takes his line in hand,
And by degrees getting the Fish to land,
Walkes to another Poole; at length is winner
Of such a dish as served him for his dinner.

W. *Browne* (*1591–1643*)

North-Country Fishing

Let your Southron stand with rod in hand,
    Fishing as in a dream,
In his one green meadow, the morning long,
    By his clear, still chalky stream;
But ever let me in the North Countree,
    Wander my burn beside,
Where it winds thro' the mead and the rocky gorge,
    And the moorland wild and wide!

They sink and they swirl, and I cannot see
    My flies, but my hand can feel,
My hands are the eyes that see the rise,
    My vision is in my reel.
Let the Southron look, like a boy, on his hook,
    For his still-stream, dimpled ring,
'Tis the hand that can *see* in the North Countree,
    And hear when the reel doth sing.

Cotswold Isys (1883)

Fishing

Fishing, if I, a fisher, may protest,
Of pleasures is the sweetest, of sports the best,
Of exercises the most excellent;
Of recreations the most innocent;
But now the sport is marde, and wott ye why?
Fishes decrease, and fishers multiply.

Thomas Bastard (1566–1618)

The Angler's Lament

Sometimes ower early,
Sometimes ower late,
Sometimes nae watter,
Sometimes a spate,
Sometimes ower thick,
And sometimes ower clear.
There's aye something wrang
When I'm fishing here.

Anonymous

The Sea-Trout
(West Highlands)

The stag to the hill
   And the bee to the clover,
The kite to his kill
   And the maid to her lover,
The bard to his dreams
   And the scribe to his cunning,
But I to the streams
   Where the sea-trout are running.

The streams of the South
   Flow in green meadow-places;
You open your mouth
   And breathe in soft graces;
Their brown trout are wise
   And take time to consider,
And you stalk every rise
   Like a hart in Balquidder.

In the North the streams flow
   With the peat running through them,
And the gods long ago
   Have hurled granite into them;
The sea-trout's a flash
   Silver sudden as laughter,
And he comes with a smash
   And considers it after.

At forty yards fair
   Off the reel he'll deliver
A leap in the air
   And a roll on the river,
And the issue's in doubt:
   Till the net's underneath him,
And he dies a sea-trout —
   Better bay could I weave him?

The loveliest – oh
  For music that I lack
To sing you his snow
  And his silver and lilac!
The wildest, the best
  And the bravest of fishes
And, however he's dressed,
  The most dainty of dishes.

But the stag to the hill
  And the bee to the clover,
The hawk to his kill
  And, a hundred times over,
My heart to the 'brow'
  In brown pools and romantic,
And the trout running through
  Off the tides of Atlantic.

  Patrick Chalmers (b. 1874)

An Angler's Rambles

I've angled far and angled wide,
On Fannich drear, by Luichart's side,
   Across dark Conan's current;
Have haunted Beauly's silver stream,
Where glimmering thro' the forest Dream
   Hangs its eternal torrent;

Among the rocks of wild Maree,
O'er whose blue billow ever free
   The daring eagles hover,
And where, at Glomach's ruffian steep,
The dark stream holds its angered leap,
   Many a fathom over;

By Lochy sad, and Laggan lake,
Where Spey uncoils his glittering snake
   Among the hills of thunder;
And I have swept my fatal fly
Where swarthy Findhorn hurries by
   The olden forest under;

On Tummel's solitary bed,
And where wild Tilt and Garry wed;
   In Athol's heathery valleys,
On Earn by green, Duneira's bower,
Below Breadalbane's Tay-washed tower,
   And Scone's once regal palace.

There have I swept the slender line,
And where the broad Awe braves the brine,
   Have watched the grey gilse gambol,
By nameless stream and tarn remote,
With light flies in the breeze afloat;
   Holding my careless ramble.

But dearer than all these to me
Is sylvan Tweed; each tower and tree
   That in its vale rejoices!
Dearer the streamlets one and all,
That blend with its Æolian brawl
   Their own enamouring voices!

Thomas Tod Stoddart (1810–1880)

Ballade of The Tweed

The *ferox* rins in rough Loch Awe,
    A weary cry frae ony toun;
The Spey, that loups o'er linn and fa',
    They praise a' ither streams aboon;
    They boast their braes o' bonny Doon:
Gie *me* to hear the ringing reel,
    Where shilfas sing and cushats croon
By fair Tweed-side, at Ashiesteel!

There's Ettrick, Meggat, Ail, and a',
    Where trout swim thick in May and June;
Ye'll see them tak' in showers o' snaw
    Some blinking, cauldrife[1] April noon:
    Rax ower the palmer and march-broun,
And syne we'll show a bonny creel,
    In spring or simmer, late or soon,
By fair Tweed-side, at Ashiesteel!

There's mony a water, great or sma',
    Gaes singing in his siller tune,
Through glen and heugh, and hope and shaw,
    Beneath the sun-licht or the moon:
    But set us in our fishing-shoon
Between the Caddon-burn and Peel,
    And syne we'll cross the heather broun
By fair Tweed-side, at Ashiesteel!

Envoy
Deil take the dirty, trading loon
    Wad gar the water ca' his wheel,
And drift his dyes and poisons doun
    By fair Tweed-side at Ashiesteel!

Andrew Lang (1844–1912)

[1] Cauldrife = chilly

Shameful Death

The biggest trout in the brook!
His weight it was five pound clear,
Never he'd wink at a hook,
If you fished for him half the year.
And in summer he lay where the tall flag shook
In the thin at the tail o' the weir.

He did not die by the line,
He did not fall to the fly,
Not fishing far and fine
On the stream where he used to lie,
But six bait-hooks and a ball o' twine
Brought that Big Trout to die.

Andrew Lang (1844–1912)

Fisher Geordie

I thocht that I was castin' steady
At the pule's tail ayont the smiddy,
Wi' finest gut and sma'est flee,
For the air was clear and the water wee;
When sudden wi' a rowst and swish
I rase a maist enormous fish....
I struck and heuked the monster shure,
Guidsakes! to see him loup in air!
It was nae saumon, na, nor troot;
To the last yaird my line gaed oot,
As up the stream the warlock ran
As wild as Job's Leviathan.
I got him stopped below the linn,
Whaur verra near I tummled in,
Aye prayin' hard my heuk wad haud;
And syne he turned a dorty jaud,
Sulkin' far down among the stanes,
I tapped the butt to stir his banes.
He warsled here and plowtered there,
But still I held him ticht and fair.
The water rinnin' exter-hie,
The sweat aye drippin' in my ee.
Sae bit by bit I wysed him richt
And broke his stieve and fashious micht,
Till sair fordone he came to book
And walloped in a shallow crook.

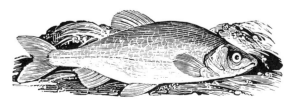

I had nae gad, sae down my wand
I flang and pinned him on the sand.
I claucht him in baith airms and peched
Ashore – he was a michty wecht;
Nor stopped till I had got his shure
Amang the threshes on the muir.
Then, Geordie lad, my een I rowed
The beast was made a' solid gowd! –
Sic ferlie as was never kenned,
A' glitterin' gowd frae end to end!
I lauched, I grat, my kep I flang,
I danced a sprig, I sang a sang.
And syne I wished that I micht dee
If wark again was touched by me....

Wi' that I woke; nae fish was there –
Juist the burnside and empty muir.

John Buchan (1875–1940)

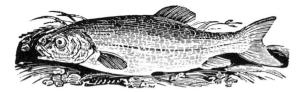

The River

Come live with me and be my love,
And we will some new pleasures prove,
Of golden sands and crystal brooks,
With silken lines and silver hooks.

There will the river whisp'ring run,
Warm'd by the eyes more than the Sun;
And there the enamell'd fish will stay,
Begging themselves they may betray.

When thou wilt swim in that live bath,
Each fish, which ev'ry channel hath,
Most am'rously to thee will swim,
Gladder to catch thee, than thou him.

If thou, to be so seen, beest loath,
By sun or moon, thou dark'ness both,
And if mine eyes have leave to see,
I need not their light, having thee.

Let others freeze with Angling-reeds,
And cut their legs with shells and weeds;
Or treach'rously poor fish beset,
With strangling snares, or windowy net.

Let coarse bold hands, from slimy nest,
The bedded fish in banks outwrest;
Let curious traitors sleave silk flies,
To 'witch poor wand'ring fishes' eyes.

For thee, thou need'st no such deceit,
For thou thyself art thine own bait:
That fish that is not catched thereby,
Is wiser far, Alas! than I.

John Donne (1572–1631)

Twilight on Tweed

Three crests against the saffron sky
  Beyond the purple plain,
The kind remembered melody
  Of Tweed once more again.

Wan water from the Border hills,
  Dear voice from the old years,
Thy distant music lulls and stills,
  And moves to quiet tears.

Like a loved ghost thy fabled flood
  Fleets through the dusky land,
Where Scott, come home to die, has stood,
  My feet returning stand.

A mist of memory broods and floats,
  The Border waters flow,
The air is full of ballad notes,
  Borne out of long ago.

Old songs that sung themselves to me,
  Sweet through a boy's day-dream,
While trout below the blossom'd tree
  Plashed in the golden stream.

Twilight, and Tweed, and Eildon Hill,
  Fair and too fair you be;
You tell me that the voice is still
  That should have welcomed me.

Andrew Lang (1844–1912)

The Angler's Song

As inward love breeds outward talk,
The hound some praise, and some the hawk,
Some, better pleas'd with private sport,
Use tennis, some a mistress court;
   But these delights I neither wish,
   Nor envy, while I freely fish.

Who hunts, doth oft in danger ride;
Who hawks, lures oft both far and wide;
Who uses games shall often prove
A loser; but who falls in love,
   Is fetter'd in fond Cupid's snare;
   My angle breeds me no such care.

Of recreation there is none
So free as fishing is alone;
All other pastimes do no less
Than mind and body both possess:
   My hand alone my work can do,
   So I can fish and study too.

I care not, I, to fish in seas,
Fresh rivers best my mind do please,
Whose sweet calm course I contemplate,
And seek in life to imitate:
   In civil bounds I fain would keep,
   And for my past offences weep.

And when the timorous Trout I wait
To take, and he devours my bait,
How poor a thing, sometimes I find,
Will captivate a greedy mind:
    And when none bite, I praise the wise
    Whom vain allurements ne'er surprise.

But yet, though while I fish, I fast,
I make good fortune my repast;
And thereunto my friend invite,
In whom I more than that delight:
    Who is more welcome to my dish
    Than to my angle was my fish.

William Basse (1602–1653)

Fisher Jamie

Puir Jamie's killed. A better lad
    Ye wadna find to busk a flee
Or burn a pule or wield a gad
    Frae Berwick to the Clints o' Dee.

And noo he's in a happier land –
    It's Gospel truith and Gospel law
That Heaven's yett maun open stand
    To folk that for their country fa'.

But Jamie will be ill to mate;
    He lo'ed nae music, kenned nae tunes
Except the sang o' Tweed in spate,
    Or Talla loupin' ower its linns.

I sair misdoot that Jamie's heid
    A crown o' gowd will never please;
He liked a kep o' dacent tweed
    Whaur he could stick his casts o' flees.

If Heaven is a' that man can dream
    And a' that honest herts can wish,
It maun provide some muirland stream,
    For Jamie dreamed o' nocht but fish.

And weel I wot he'll up and speir
    In his bit blate and canty way,
Wi' kind Apostles standin' near
    Whae in their time were fishers tae.

He'll offer back his gowden croun
    And in its place a rod he'll seek,
And bashful-like his herp lay down
    And speir a leister and a cleek.

For Jims had aye a poachin' whim;
  He'll sune grow tired, wi' lawfu' flee
Made frae the wings o' cherubim,
  O' castin' ower the Crystal Sea....

I picter him at gloamin' tide
  Steekin' the backdoor o' his hame
And hastin' to the waterside
  To play again the auld auld game;

And syne wi' saumon on his back,
  Catch't clean against the Heavenly law,
And Heavenly byliffs on his track,
  Gaun linkin' doun some Heavenly shaw.

John Buchan (1875–1940)

The Devout Angler

The years will bring their anodyne,
  But I shall never quite forget
The fish that I had counted mine
  And lost before they reached the net.

Last night I put my rod away
  Remorseful and disconsolate,
Yet I had suffered yesterday
  No more than I deserved from Fate.

And as I scored another trout
    Upon my list of fish uncaught,
I should have offered thanks, no doubt,
    For salutary lessons taught.

Alas! Philosophy avails
    As little as it used to do.
More comfort is there still in tales
    That may be, or may not, be true.

Is it not possible to pray
    That I may see those fish once more?
I hear a voice that seems to say,
    'They are not lost but gone before.'

When in my pilgrimage I reach
    The river that we all must cross,
And land upon that further beach
    Where earthly gains are counted loss,

May I not earthly loss repair?
    Well, if those fish should rise again,
There shall be no more parting there –
    Celestial gut will stand the strain.

And issuing from the portal, one
    Who was himself a fisherman
Will drop his keys and, shouting, run
    To help me land Leviathan.

Colin Ellis (1889–1969)

The Taking Of The Salmon

A Birr! a whirr! a salmon's on,
  A goodly fish! a thumper!
Bring up, bring up the ready gaff,
And if we land him we shall quaff
  Another glorious bumper!
    Hark! 'tis the music of the reel,
      The strong, the quick, the steady;
    The line darts from the active wheel,
      Have all things right and ready.

A birr! a whirr! the salmon's out,
  Far on the rushing river;
Onward he holds with sudden leap,
Or plunges through the whirlpool deep,
  A desperate endeavour!
    Hark to the music of the reel!
      The fitful and the grating:
    It pants along the breathless wheel,
      Now hurried – now abating.

A birr! a whirr! the salmon's off!
  No, no, we still have got him;
The wily fish is sullen grown,
And, like a bright imbedded stone,
  Lies gleaming at the bottom.
    Hark to the music of the reel!
      'Tis hush'd, it hath forsaken;
    With care we'll guard the magic wheel,
      Until its notes rewaken.

A birr! a whirr! the salmon's up,
  Give line, give line and measure;
But now he turns! keep down ahead,
And lead him as a child is led
  And land him at your leisure.

Hark to the music of the reel!
  'Tis welcome, it is glorious;
It wanders thro' the winding wheel,
  Returning and victorious.

A birr! a whirr! the salmon's in,
  Upon the bank extended;
The princely fish is gasping slow,
His brilliant colours come and go,
  All beautifully blended.
    Hark to the music of the reel!
      It murmurs and it closes;
    Silence is on the conquering wheel,
      Its wearied line reposes.

No birr! no whirr! the salmon's ours,
  The noble fish – the thumper:
Strike through his gill the ready gaff,
And bending homewards, we shall quaff
  Another glorious bumper!
    Hark to the music of the reel!
      We listen with devotion;
    There's something in that circling wheel
      That wakes the heart's emotion!

Thomas Tod Stoddart (1810–1880)

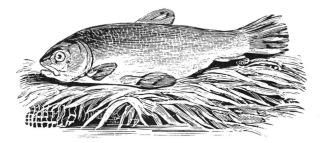

The Angler's Vindication

Say not our hands are cruel;
    What deeds invite the blame?
Content our golden jewel,
    No blemish on our name:
        Creation's lords
        We need no swords
    To win a withering fame.

Say not in gore and guile
    We waste the livelong day;
Let those alone revile
    Who feel our subtile sway,
        When fancy-led
        The sward we tread
    And while the morn away.

Oh! not in camp or court
    Our best delights we find,
But in the far resort
    With water, wood, and wind,
        Where Nature works
        And beauty lurks
    In all her craft enshrined.

There captive to her will
    Yet, 'mid our fetters free,
We seek by singing rill
    The broad and shady tree,
        And lisp our lay
        To flower and fay,
    Or mock the linnet's glee.

Thus glides the golden hour,
  Under the chimes to toil
Recall from brook and bower:
  Then laden with our spoil,
    Slowly we part
    With heavy heart
And leave the haunted soil.

Thomas Tod Stoddart (1810–1880)

Heaven

Fish (fly-replete, in depth of June
Dawdling away their wat'ry noon)
Ponder deep wisdom, dark or clear,
Each secret fishy hope or fear.
Fish say, they have their Stream and Pond;
But is there anything Beyond?
This cannot be All, they swear,
For how unpleasant, if it were!
One may not doubt that, somehow, good
Shall come of Water and of Mud;
And, sure, the reverent eye must see
A Purpose in Liquidity.
We darkly know, by Faith we cry,
The future is not Wholly Dry.
Mud unto Mud! – Death eddies near –
Not here the appointed End, not here!
But somewhere, beyond Space and Time,
In wetter water, slimier slime!
And there (they trust) there swimmeth One
Who swam ere rivers were begun,
Immense of fishy form and mind,
Squamous, omnipotent, and kind;
And under the Almighty Fin
The littlest fish may enter in.
Oh! never fly conceals a hook,
Fish say, in the Eternal Brook,
But more than mundane weeds are there,
And mud, celestially fair;
Fat caterpillars drift around,
And Paradisal grubs are found;
Unfading moths, immortal flies,
And the worm that never dies.
And in that Heaven of all their wish,
There shall be no more land, say fish.

Rupert Brooke (1887–1915)

The River

Through the sun-bright lakes,
  Round islets gay,
The river takes
  Its western way,
And the water-chime
Soft zephyrs time
  Each gladsome summer day.

The starry trout,
  Fair to behold,
Roameth about
  On fin of gold;
At root of tree
His haunt you see,
  Rude rock or crevice old.

And hither dart
  The salmon grey,
From the deep heart
  Of some sea bay;
And harling wild
Is here beguiled
  To hold autumnal play.

Oh! 'tis a stream
  Most fair to see
As in a dream
  Flows pleasantly;
And our hearts are woo'd
To a kind sweet mood
  By its wondrous witchery.

Thomas Tod Stoddart (*1810–1880*)

Epitaph

God grant that I may fish
Until my dying day.
And when it comes to my last cast,
I humbly pray.
When in the Lord's landing net
I'm peacefully asleep
That in his mercy
I be judged as good enough to keep.

Charles John Fitzroy Rhys Wingfield
in Great Barrington Church, Oxfordshire

SHOOTING

BOOK III

A Father's Advice to His Son

If a sportsman true you'd be,
Listen carefully to me.

Never, never let your gun
Pointed be at anyone;
That it may unloaded be
Matters not the least to me.

When a hedge or fence you cross,
Though of time it cause a loss,
From your gun the cartridge take,
For the greater safety's sake.

If t'wixt you and neighbouring gun
Birds may fly or beasts may run,
Let this maxim e'er be thine:
FOLLOW NOT ACROSS THE LINE.

Stops and beaters oft unseen
Lurk behind some leafy screen;
Calm and steady always be:
NEVER SHOOT WHERE YOU CAN'T SEE.

Keep your place and silent be:
Game can hear and game can see;
Don't be greedy, better spared
Is a pheasant than one shared.

You may kill or you may miss,
But at all times think of this:
All the pheasants ever bred
Won't repay for one man dead.

Mark Beaufoy

Lord Lucky

Lord Lucky, by a curious fluke,
Became a most important duke.
From living in a vile Hotel
A long way east of Camberwell
He rose, in less than half an hour,
To riches, dignity and power.
It happened in the following way: –
The Real Duke went out one day
To shoot with several people, one
Of whom had never used a gun.
This gentleman (a Mr Meyer
Of Rabley Abbey, Rutlandshire),
As he was scrambling through the brake,
Discharged his weapon by mistake,
And plugged about an ounce of lead
Piff-bang into his Grace's Head –
Who naturally fell down dead.
His Heir, Lord Ugly, roared, 'You Brute!
Take that to teach you how to shoot!'
Whereat he volleyed, left and right;
But being somewhat short of sight
His right-hand Barrel only got
The second heir, Lord Poddleplot;
The while the left-hand charge (or choke)
Accounted for another bloke,
Who stood with an astounded air
Bewildered by the whole affair
– And was the third remaining heir.
After the Execution (which
Is something rare among the Rich)
Lord Lucky, while of course he needed
Some help to prove his claim, succeeded.
– But after his succession, though
All this was over years ago,
He only once indulged the whim
Of asking Meyer to lunch with him.

Hilaire Belloc (1870–1953)

The Five Marks

Five gen'ral sorts of *Flying Marks* there are;
The *Lineals* two, *Traverse* and *Circular*;
The Fifth *Oblique*, which I may vainly teach;
But Practice only perfectly can reach.

When a Bird comes directly to your Face,
Contain your Fire awhile, and let her pass,
Unless some Trees behind you change the Case.
If so, a little space above her Head
Advance the Muzzle, and you strike her dead.
Ever let Shot pursue where there is room;
Marks, hard before, thus easy will become.

But, when the Bird flies from you in a line
With little Care, I may pronounce her thine.
Observe the Rule before, and neatly raise
Your piece, till there's no *Open Under-Space*
Betwixt the Object and the *Silver Sight*;
Then send away, and timely stop the Flight.

Th'unlucky *Cross Mark*, or the *Traverse Shoot*,
By some thought easy, yet admits Dispute,
As the most common Practice is, to Fire
Before the Bird, will nicest time require:
For, too much Space allow'd, the Shot will fly
All innocent, and pass too nimbly by;
Too little Space, the Partridge swift as Wind,
Will dart athwart, and bilk her Death behind.
This makes the Point so difficult to guess;
'Cause you must be exact in Time, or miss.
Where the swift Shot will sure *Overtake*;

Nor need the Sportsman such strict Measures make:
And better will the *Lineal Aim* allow
A Hundred Inches, than the *Cross Mark* Two.

Full Forty Yards, or more to th'Left or Right,
The Partridge then *Obliquely* takes her Flight.
You've there th'Advantage of a *Sideling Line*,
Be careful, nor her inward side decline:
Else just behind the Bird the Shot will glance:
Nor have you any Hopes from *Flying Chance*.

Thus in the Mark which is stil'd *Circular*,
There's nothing more requir'd, but steady care
T'attend the Motion of the Bird, and gain
The best and farthest *Lineal Point* you can;
Carrying your Piece around, have Patience till
The Mark's at best Extent, then fire and kill.

George Markland

Neither Too Soon Nor Too Late

There sprung a single Partridge – ha! she's gone!
Oh! Sir, you'd Time enough, you shot too soon;
Scarce Twenty Yards in open Sight! – for Shame!
Y'had shattered Her to Pieces with right Aim!
Full Forty Yards permit the Bird to go,
The spreading Gun will surer Mischief sow;
But, when too near the flying Object is,
You certainly will mangle it, or miss;
And if too far, you may so slightly wound,
To kill the Bird, and yet not bring to Ground.

George Markland

The Companyes of Bestys and Foule

An Herde of swannys
An Herde of cranys
An Herde of corlewys
An Herde of wrennys
A Nye of fesauntys
A Bevy of quayles
A Sege of herons
A Sege of bytourys
A Sorde or a Sute of malards
A Mustre of pecockys
A Walke of snytes
An Exaltynge of larkys
A Cherme of golfynches
A Flyghte of dovves
An Unkyndnes of ravens
A Clayterynge of choughes
A Dyssymulacion of byrdes
A Bevy of conyes
A Cowple of spanellys
A Tryppe of haarys
A Gagle of geys
A Brode of hennys
A Badelynge of dokys
A Covy of pertryches
A Sprynge of telys[1]

A Deseerte of lapwynges
A Falle of wodcockes
A Congregacion of plovers
A Coverte of cootes
A Duell of turtylles
A Tygendis of pyes
A Flyght of swalowes
A Buyldynge of rokys
A Murmuracion of stares[2]
A Nest of rabettys.

Dame Juliana Berners (1486) The Boke of St. Albans

1 Telys = teals
2 Stares = starlings

To a Cock Pheasant

Good morrow, good morrow, Sir Knight of the mail
   That's bronze and that's copper, that's collared a-ring;
From the tip of your beak to the tip of your tail
You're splendid as Autumn ablaze in the vale;
King Solomon's glory before you would pale
   As you strut in the ride like a king.

A whistle behind you, a whistle, d'you hear?
   And, anon, a tip-tapping of stick upon stock
Will you slip (in strategic retreat) to the rear?
Well, you haven't been shot at, I fancy, this year,
So you'll act in the royaler way, never fear,
   And rise with a raucous *cok-cok!*

A phoenix you'll rise through the tops, still afire,
   Still aflame with the season's resplendent decay;
A phoenix that springs from a funeral pyre
Of oakwoods in ember, and straight doth aspire
To the frosty bright blue, to the blue you require
   To show off your fireworkish way.

Then forward you'll swing (like a comet at need
   Of Olympian Zeus), gaining pace as you go;
High, high o'er the branches (*cock forward!*) you'll speed
Till you're clear of the cover, a screamer indeed,
And out o'er the meadow; but, mark you, take heed
   Of those odd little groups far below.

They're the Guns, the adepts, as you'll presently see;
   Myself (on the flank) cut a figure to mock
With artists of *their* sort; at full apogee
Approach them, professors in highest degree,
Accomplished to 'larn' you most deftly to be
   A pheasant and, more so, a cock!

But beaters are coming; *tap*, *tap*, down the breeze
   Their sticks get the nearer, so up in your pride
In Autumn's gold sunshine, high o'er her gold trees,
Till, tall as the tallest, you sail at your ease;
And 'tis best to be tall, tall as Troy an you please,
   When those batteries open outside.

   Patrick Chalmers (*b. 1874*)

Birds That Abound in Scotland

The lakes and mountains swarm with copious game;
The wildgoose gray, and heathcock hairy-legg'd,
White soland, that on Bass and Ailsa build;
The woodcock slender billed, and marshy snipe,
The free-bred duck, that scorns the wiles of men,
Soaring beyond the thunder of the gun;
Yet oft her crafty fellow, trained to guile,
And forging love, decoys her to the snare,
There witnesses her fate, with shameless brow.
Why should I here the fruitful pigeon name,
Or long-necked heron, dread of nimble eels,
The glossy swan, that loaths to look a-down,
Or the close covey vexed with various woes?
While sad, they sit their anxious mother round,
With dismal shade the closing net descends;
Or, by the sudden gun, they fluttering fall,
And vile with blood, is stained their freckled down.

J. Leyden (1775–1811)

The First Drive

A diamond the morn is set,
  So clear, so blue, so bright,
Though in the shade, a sparkle yet,
  Lurks rime from overnight;
Men name such morns the ember days
  Of leaf and stricken bower,
Yet colour sets the wood a-blaze,
  Yet colour rules the hour.

We wait behind the blackthorn hedge,
  The beaters' slow advance;
Gold sedges hold the sun in pledge,
  A finch's gold wings glance;
Faint-calling partridges afar...
  My son, in briefest words,
The roots beyond the stubbles are
  Fair chock-a-block with birds.

Just now a stoat ran through the thorn,
  Red, evilly he ran,
A murderous brute for such a morn,
  But so mayhap's a man;
'Neath skies of spun forget-me-nots
  Ere minutes ten be sped
I look to fire a score of shots,
  To kill, I hope, ten head.

Ah, here they come! The first lot springs
  Aloft and skims adown
The stubble with a flick of wings,
  Quick swerving, trim and brown;
Now, ere they cross the space between,
  Now, Dian, grant me this,
That, where I hit, I kill 'em clean,
  That, when I miss, I miss.

Patrick Chalmers (b. 1874)

Wild Geese

They're shy as the otter, they're sly as the fox,
They're worse to approach than the craftiest hind,
You may freeze on the fore-shore or crouch on the rocks,
You may soak in the sea-fog or wait in the wind,
Though their magical music will give you no peace,
Yet your bag shall go empty, for aren't they wild geese?

Honk-honk, honk-honk, the distant voices clank it;
The wet retriever trembles at your knee;
  For he hears the lone notes falling,
  Where the long grey tides are crawling,
Through the shouting west wind's buffets or the dripping fog's
    chill blanket,
As the wild geese come shoreward from the sea!

You may stalk them at sundown, at dawning's first flame,
They've ears for the wariest, softest of treads,
And, stook-time or snow-time, the end is the same
A picket gives warning and up go their heads;
Yes, your boots (wet as sponges in spite of their grease)
You may wear to brown paper in chasing wild geese.

Yet still, *honk-honk*, a northern charm shall fold you
Though Shot shall shake the raindrops from his sides
  Though you catch the drifting clamour
  Through the sleet squall's sting and hammer,
Still the flight shall work its magic and the breathless stalk shall
    hold you,
When the grey geese come calling off the tides!

Patrick Chalmers (b. 1874)

The Crime

On the First of September, one Sunday morn,
I shot a hen pheasant in standing corn
Without a licence. Contrive who can
Such a cluster of crimes against God and man!

Richard Monckton, First Lord Houghton (1809–1885)

Noon

Enough! Enough! no longer we pursue
The scattered covey in the tainted dew.
No more we charge, nor new excursions make,
Nor beat the copse, the bean-field, nor the brake.
O pleasing sport! far better prized than wealth!
Thou spring of spirits, and thou source of health,
Thou giv'st, when thus our leisure we employ,
To life the relish and the zest to joy,
O may I still on rural pleasures bent,
Rove devious in sequester'd fields of Kent;
Ease, study, exercise successive blend,
Nor want the blessing of a cheerful friend!

Forbear, my dogs! now mid-day heats prevail,
The scent grows languid in the sultry gale;
Herds seek the shades where cooling fountains well,
And sweet the music of your noon-tide bell.

Francis Fawkes (1720–1777)

The Wild Duck

Twilight. Red in the west.
Dimness. A glow on the wood.
The teams plod home to rest.
The wild duck come to glean.
O souls not understood,
What wild cry in the pool;
What things have the farm ducks seen
That they cry so-huddle and cry?

Only the soul that goes.
Eager. Eager. Flying.
Over the globe of the moon,
Over the wood that glows,
Wings linked. Necks a-strain,
A rush and a wild crying.

    *   *   *   *

A cry of the long pain
In the reeds of a steel lagoon,
In a land that no man knows.

John Masefield (1878–1967)

Snipe Shooting

When gelid frosts encrust the faded ground,
And dreary winter clouds the scene around;
The timid snipes fly to the sedgy rills,
Or seek the plashes on the upland hills.
The sportsman, now, wakes with the gleaming morn,
His gun makes fit, refills his pouch and horn,
And to the swampy meadow takes his way,
With sport and exercise to crown the day.
See first how curiously he scans the sedge,
Then warily proceeds along the edge:
His piece is cock'd, and in position right,
To meet his shoulder readily and light.
But yet more cautiously he treads beside
The well-known plash, where most he thinks do hide
The dappled bird – and from the rushy stream.
His tube the fowler points with steady sight,
And seeks to trace her thro' her rapid flight;
Whilst o'er the field she tries each artful wile,
And crooked turn, his level to beguile.
Her slender wings swift cut the buoyant air,
'Till distance gives her as a mark more fair:
Now glancing, just the marksman gets his aim,
His ready finger doth the trigger strain.
He fires – the fatal shot unerring flies,
The snipe is struck, she flutters, bleeds, and dies.

'Sporting Magazine' (1798)

Philosophy in the Butt

Moved by the beauty of the scene,
   While in my butt I wait,
Against my fringe of sods I lean
   My gun and meditate:
What solitude, what glorious air,
   What peace and quiet everywhere!

I see the russet heather sweep
   That stretches to the sky,
I see the wandering mountain sheep
   That trip demurely by;
I see against the cloudless blue
   The beaters rising into view.

Surely it were a graceless act
   On this delightful day,
Of man, to seek this moorland tract
   To desolate and slay,
An act of massacre – and, hark!
   I hear a distant shout of 'Mark!'

'Mark over,' and I mark black specks,
   Which into grouse increase;
Like one whom no misgivings vex
   I lay my ruthless piece;
Bang! bang! the pack skims by unharmed,
   Not even, it would seem, alarmed.

Here comes another lot full tilt
   Towards the dangerous goal;
Both barrels do not fix the guilt
   Of murder on my soul:
Courageous birds, all undismayed
   By my alarming fusillade.

The beaters come: so ends the drive,
 Jones claims his usual brace,
Stolid professional dogs arrive
 And sniff about the place:
They set to work with what I feel
Is likely to be wasted zeal.

By Smith's authority empowered
 We seek a far-off spot,
Where, as he says, a quarry towered
 Sore-smitten by his shot:
We take immense, though futile pains
About retrieving the remains.

So my preliminary sighs
 Were out of place, I see:
A saving preposition lies
 'Twixt massacre and me:
Mine is an innocent pursuit.
I shoot at – but I do not shoot.

Alfred Cochrane (b. 1865)

The Last Drive

The gales are gotten up with night,
    The stormy West's a-hum,
And hardly there'll be shooting light
    To last till beaters come;
I hear a grouse-cock's wild 'Go Back,'
    I see a kindling star
Redden amid the flying wrack
    Above the braes of Mar.

Oh, different, different was it once,
    One 'walked,' in August's prime,
Convenient coveys which a dunce
    Could deal with every time;
Are they the self-same birds, indeed,
    That, this late afternoon,
Come, like the levin and will need
    A *man* to 'ca' them doun'?

But look, a lot's aloft and on,
    A whistle bids us mark;
Cowards, curling from the butts, they're gone
    Across the wind and dark;
Again, again – *these* shall not shirk,
    They're here a headlong cloud,
And, crackling through the gusty mirk,
    The batteries bark aloud.

And yet again, and yet again,
    Till last one single spy,
Like thunderbolt of Jove, amain
    Hurls through the darkening sky;
Hold yards ahead, and *yards* ahead,
    And breathe a prayer to Pan...
He crumples and he crashes, dead
    As Cæsar or Queen Anne.

The last, indeed, the finished tale;
  The dogs are picking up;
While dusk, upon the gathering gale,
  Fills glen and corrie's cup;
Fair days, fair days, your sum's complete,
  'Tis Southward ho! to Town;
Yet was your end most fair and feat –
  Nine shots and seven down!

Patrick Chalmers (b. 1874)

The Perennial Rabbit

The savage by primeval Thames,
Lurking, the mammoth to waylay,
Amid the awful forest stems,
On some far, dim, forgotten day,
As the vast bulk of brawn and beef
Squelched off unscathed through lone morasses,
Would turn, I doubt not, with relief
To where you scuttled in the grasses!

Perhaps my cave-man blood's to blame,
For – atavistic taint – I too
Have dropped a more exacting game,
Bunny, to have a bang at you;
The driven partridge missed in front,
And eke behind, lacks serious merit
Beside a sunny hedgerow hunt,
A terrier and an active ferret!

Give me a summer afternoon,
An air-gun and the drone of bees,
The water-meadows lush with June,
A stalk among the Alderneys;
Then, hit or miss, I care no-ways,
In such surroundings I consider
You're worth a hundred storm-swept braes
And all the royals in Balquidder!

Indeed, wherever I may go,
Through summer woods, by wintry fell,
I've found you, in the sun or snow,
A friendly little Ishmael;
Along the southern trout-stream banks,
Or with the ptarmigan consorting,
You've always earned my grateful thanks,
And in all seasons acted sporting!

Hushed is the hairy Mammoth's roar
And gone the mastodon uncouth
Down to decay with dinosaur,
Aurochs, and fearsome sabre-tooth;
But you, small beast in hodden-gray,
Survive, and will, I take for granted,
Be here when I am dust, to play
In moonlit covers still unplanted.

Patrick Chalmers (b. 1874)

The Lincolnshire Polcher

When I was bound apprentice in fair *Lincolnshire*,
Full well I served my master for more than seven year,
'Till I took up to *polching*, as you shall quickly hear,
O 'tis my delight, in a shining night, in the season of the year.

As me and my *comrade* were setting of a snare,
'Twas then we spied the game-keeper – for him we did not care.
For we can wrestle and fight, my boys, and jump o'er anywhere.
O 'tis my delight, on a shining night, in the season of the year.

As me and my *comrade* were setting four or five,
And taking on them up again we caught the hare alive,
We caught the hare alive, my boys, and through the woods did steer.
O 'tis my delight on a shining night, in the season of the year.

We throdun him over our shoulder, and then we trudged home,
We took him to a neighbour's house and sold him for a crown,
We sold him for a crown, my boys, but I did not tell you where,
O 'tis my delight on a shining night, in the season of the year.

Success to every gentleman that lives in Lincolnshire,
Success to every *polcher* that wants to sell a hare,
Bad luck to every game-keeper that will not sell his deer.
O 'tis my delight on a shining night, in the season of the year.

Old Song

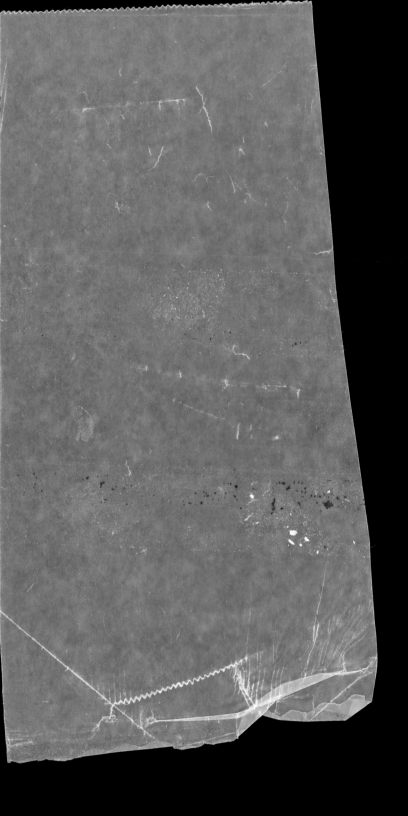

Poaching in Excelsis

'Two men were fined £120 apiece for poaching a white rhinoceros.' SOUTH AFRICAN PRESS

I've poached a pickle paitricks[1] when the leaves were turnin' sere,
I've poached a twa-three hares an' grouse, an' mebbe whiles a
    deer,
But ou, it seems an unco[2] thing, an' jist a wee mysterious,
Hoo any mortal could contrive tae poach a rhinocerious.

I've crackit[3] wi' the keeper, pockets packed wi' pheasants eggs,
An' a ten-pun' saumon hangin' doun in baith my trouser legs,
But he, I doot effects wud be a wee thing deleterious
Gin ye shuld stow intil yer breeks a brace o'rhinocerious.

I mind hoo me an' Wullie shot a Royal in Braemar,
An' brocht him doun tae Athol by the licht o'mune an' star.
An' eh, Sirs! but the canny beast contrived tae fash an' weary
    us –
Yet staigs maun be but bairn's play besides a rhinocerious.

I thocht I kent o' poachin' just as muckle's ither men,
But there is still a twa-three things I doot I dinna ken;
An' noo I cannot rest, my brain is growin' that deleerious
Tae win awa' tae Africa an' poach a rhinocerious.

    G. K. Menzies

---

1 Pickle paitricks = small quantity of
2 Unco = strange
3 Crackit = talked

The Old Gamekeeper

In actual years I understand
    That he is turned of sixty-seven,
His rugged brows are seamed and tanned
    With all the winds and suns of heaven;
Yet, though about his beard and hair
    Old Time has scattered snow in plenty,
He fronts you with a stalwart air,
    As upright as a lad of twenty.

A patriarch this of gun and rod,
    Of gaff and fly, of fur and feather,
Who upon fifty Twelfths has trod
    With Don and Rambler through the heather:
Who as a round-eyed urchin stared
    At older squires in strange apparel,
And can recall the present laird
    A novice with a single barrel.

Year in, year out, his lot is cast
    In none but outdoor occupation;
Before his patient eyes goes past
    The changeless pageant of creation;
Year out, year in, the garnered sheaf,
    The frost-bound earth, the April shower,
The mystery of the bursting leaf,
    The nesting thrush, the budding flower.

On many a fragrant night of May,
    All silver-white in moonlit beauty,
He waits and watches till the day,
    A patient devotee of duty;
While past the pines the brown owl swoops
    With silent wings and ghostly sailings,
He stands to guard the pheasant coops,
    His back against the spinney railings.

A more romantic sentry might,
    On some delightful revel chancing,
Have seen in the soft summer night
    Great Pan amid his Dryads dancing;
But his calm wits would not expect
    So false and pagan an *imago*,
While he is wondering what effect
    The dew will have on his lumbago.

In days when courtesy is dim,
    And speech grown less polite and plainer
You never fail to find in him
    The deference of the old retainer;
He speaks about the crops and birds,
    About the weather and the stubbles,
With some apologetic words
    Of stiffness and rheumatic troubles.

With here and there a humorous touch,
    Of which you catch a distant inkling,
And guess that it is meant as such
    Because his honest eyes are twinkling;
Then back to more professional ground,
    To beats and spaniels, guns and setters.
As if herein alone he found
    Fit conversation for his betters.

Yet among more familiar friends,
    With nothing to suggest disparity,
Rumour reports that he unbends,
    To prodigies of jocularity;
Nay, when the reels and jigs begin,
    At Hallowe'en or Twelfth Night party,
Upon an ancient violin
    He scrapes a self-taught Sarasate.

Exciting stories, too, he tells,
  Great feats of memory or invention,
And round the dying fire compels
  The listening harness-room's attention:
With moving anecdotes of sport,
  Of midnight raid and poaching battle,
Or else, the more exciting sort,
  Of ghosts that walk and chains that rattle.

I wonder if we joined the crowd
  If he would pardon our intrusion,
Would he continue and be proud,
  Or would we fill him with confusion?
I dare not risk it: I must be
  His comrade through the heather plodding,
To whom it is not given to see
  This Homer of the gun-room nodding.

Alfred Cochrane (b. 1865)

The Dead Gamekeeper

Earth now holds him in her rooty snare
   Beneath the rat-run sycamore;
Far is fur and feather from his care,
   Another watcher lifts his door.

Now vermilion-fanged the vermin dare
   Creep out from fosse and fen and cave;
And the wild hawks on the flowing air
   Poise and pass above his grave.

Anonymous

Acknowledgments

The author and publisher would like to thank the following for permission to reproduce certain copyright poems:
Hilaire Belloc, *Lord Epsom* and *Lord Lucky*, from MORE PEERS. Reprinted by permission of Gerald Duckworth & Co Ltd.
John Betjeman, *Hunter Trials*, from COLLECTED POEMS. Reprinted by permission of the author and John Murray (Publishers) Ltd.
John Buchan, *Fisher Geordie* and *Fisher Jamie*, from POEMS SCOTS AND ENGLISH. Reprinted by permission of the Estate of John Buchan.
Patrick Chalmers, *The Sea Trout (West Highlands)* from PIPES AND TABORS, and *The Unattainable*, *Wild Geese* and *The Perennial Rabbit* from GREEN DAYS AND BLUE DAYS. Reprinted by permission of Methuen & Co Ltd.
The Last Drive by Patrick Chalmers is reprinted by permission of *Punch*.
Alfred Cochrane, *Philosophy in the Butt*, from COLLECTED VERSES (1903) and *The Old Gamekeeper*, from LATER VERSES (1918). Reprinted by permission of the Longman Group Ltd.
Walter de la Mare, *The Fish*, from STUFF AND NONSENSE. Reprinted by permission of Constable & Co Ltd.
Colin Ellis, *The Devout Angler*, from MOURNFUL NUMBERS. Reprinted by permission of Macmillan, London and Basingstoke.
John Masefield, *The Wild Duck*. Reprinted by permission of the Society of Authors as the literary representative of the Estate of John Masefield.
Edric Roberts, *The Whip*. Reprinted by permission of Constable & Co Ltd.

Every effort has been made to discover the owners of copyright material reprinted. On receiving notification, any omissions that have occurred will be rectified.

Index of Authors